MAYBE THE BODY

"*Maybe the Body* is a radiant collection, a generous offering full of flora and fury, plums, and caterpillars. These poems are a field of inheritance where language, history, and lineage collide, and in Drake's capable hands, the body becomes both question and altar."

—**AIMEE NEZHUKUMATATHIL**,
bestselling author of
World of Wonders and *Oceanic*

"'Sometimes, history is too beautiful to be believed,' Asa Drake writes in her collection *Maybe the Body*, which is an extensive love song of memory, family, self, and the challenges of differentiating one from the other. When a speaker wades in a river that runs beneath an interstate, they think of a mother's words: 'Care first. Decide about love later.' This book is about places and homes: ones we don't want to lose, ones we find in others, and those we must decide to build for ourselves. *Maybe the Body* is the home I have longed for."

—**PHILLIP B. WILLIAMS**,
author of *Mutiny* and *Ours*

"To inhabit the pages of the deeply introspective *Maybe the Body* is to 'walk / through the valley of semblance.' Here, investigation and insight lie in the backhanded compliment, the letter of resignation, the shifting landscape in a storm, the microaggression, the I love you, the surcharge, and the moments of transcription and erasure. Every poem perches resolutely on the hyphen, the intersection in a Venn diagram. This collection debuts Asa Drake as a sage of liminal states and spaces."

—**JANINE JOSEPH**,
author of *Decade of the Brain*

MAYBE THE BODY

POEMS

ASA DRAKE

Tin House

Tin House is an imprint of Zando.
zandoprojects.com

First US Edition 2026
Manufacturing by Kingery Printing Company
Text and cover design by Beth Steidle

Library of Congress Control Number is available.

978-1-963108-68-2 (paperback)
978-1-963108-76-7 (ebook)

10 9 8 7 6 5 4 3 2 1

Manufactured in the United States of America

for Viwa and Eda

CONTENTS

It was helpful for me to understand camouflage
as not a tactic of war, but a way in which a
body can occupy an out-of-body space.
—GINA OSTERLOH

I will plant companionship thick as trees along
all the rivers of America, and along the shores
of the great lakes, and all over the prairies,
I will make inseparable cities
—"FOR YOU O DEMOCRACY," WALT WHITMAN

MAYBE THE BODY

TO SOMEONE WHO'S HEARD *I LOVE YOU* TOO MANY TIMES

The couple who owns the restaurant that makes
you feel safe with homemade bean curd uses a variation,
I love your—and the stipulation of achievability—
you would have such beautiful children. So many people
are interested in how you may multiply, even if puberty
made you cry. The way a parent says, *I love you*,
to their half of your body (or do they address
the parent they loved whose recessive lack of underarm hair
lives on as a party trick? Every time you undress,
your lola enters the bedroom with you). That special
mestiza mystique which a friend bemoans
belongs to some mestizas and not others. She doesn't know
another way to say, *I love you*.

1

In 1981, Tita Nena translates Whitman to make a primer for revolution. My mother has just left Quezon City. I am not yet born. In some versions of her departure, santols roll down a blue tarp onto Nanay's balcony for a century without translation. Neighbors develop ways to predict when my mother returns. Like rain during procession.

This is the part of me I must show everyone first.

CERTAIN OUTLINES CAN ONLY BE IMAGINED

Rain overflowing from the cup
I left outside. Honestly, it's the wrong year
to write a love poem. Though I walk
through the valley of semblance
I am every figure in the deck. Magnolias
make me feel guilty. Half I go where
my mother sends me, half I deliver
unintended messages. Chimera
of passionflowers running into Lady Banks
barely keeping pace with the sampaguitas.
How Lady Banks is a placeholder name
for the unknown gardener who tended
this cultivar in China before 1807.
By *placeholder*, I mean *erasure*
but I would like to mean *placeholder*.
I would like—one day—
for the gardener to be revealed.

Sometimes the thing that may destroy
your home sings. I love that song too.

Room for uncertainty.

Make room in yourself for the longest sentence
you have yet to say. That was my only singing lesson.

For safety, I abandoned any clothes preoccupied with language, even
a dry rotted rice sack

with the word *sweet.* Even hair clips inscribed
with clarity: *don't* and *touch.*

Today, I looked for the smallest iteration of myself.

I am thinking of ordering plums from California
because at this moment they are on the tree

and at 11 a.m. they will not. I am in love
with this kind of transparency.

Room for uncertainty.

A friend reads fortunes in my hair when my lover won't, love
refracted between us to make everyone in the room more beautiful.

And still, someone enters to ask if I wasn't born lucky.
I keep a whole rabbit to help me survive. Oh, it eats

and eats at what I was born with. Beloved, if I titled this poem
“My Mother’s America,” would it contain her mother? How long

before you know the urgency of this sentence is lost?

TO SOMEONE WHO'S HEARD *I LOVE YOU* TOO MANY TIMES

Another way of saying *I love you* involves
what a lover promises
as you wash your face in the sink. This morning,
that was good for me. The first or the second
or the third best thing will happen.
The pet with bad poops will live.
I want to forget why I am here
in the first place and slide my foot under
the rabbit's extrasoft belly. This isn't solely pleasure;
I'm feeling for the death bubble. The sound
that means an animal is working vs. the sound
I have yet to hear. A death scream
I heard once in college meant
I fell out of love with whomever
I had previously loved. A sound altered my heart.

DISAGREEABLE ASPECTS OF HYPHENATION

Driving through the South wearing my mother's clothes vs. someone who visits like they don't know how to approach a wasp nest.

A coworker explains there's nothing special about the food I grew up with. I had invited her into my home. I had picked fruit from my own yard, food I'd grown because it was impossible to buy. She had packed a to-go plate for her husband.

That's when she, leaving, told me, *There's nothing special about the food you grew up with.*

I forget to protect my teeth, and now I find craze lines in the enamel.

The webinar trainer asks that I practice. *What are you going to say?*

It is so easy to know how another will root out my provenance. Less to understand what I want from this conversation I don't want.

I don't know.

To protect my teeth, I put my tongue between the bite.

It's been twenty-four years, and I still carry a nest of small animals. This year's is the first that survives. Something I've touched that lives, so this is the least of my sins.

I don't think the dead are waiting for us to do anything in particular.

Remember, America is only one possibility.

Online, the silk advertises I can sleep anywhere and shows me bodies asleep in the desert. Here the snakes don't bite. They wrap around me under a silk gown and keep their mouths closed. Keeping our mouths closed keeps us warm. Dreaming a man—not the lover—gets too close, so close we all open our mouths.

Who's happier than Medusa? I think I hear my lover, but I've misheard him. He was cutting her up. *Who's halved more than Medusa?*

I can't say.

There are a million things you can halve in the world. A million you can't.

HEIRLOOM

I never asked my mother what she brought with her
but by the time she left home, she had $20. My father, too. A magic currency

that cuts a life in two. No wonder all my life
they pressed large bills in my hand. When summarizing events unfortunate/
fortunate,

fortunate appears twice. I want to know whether this changes the record.
I like to watch videos of this aging rabbit on Instagram being hand-fed parsley

and sliced apples because of what this implies about our capacity
for love. This skin-mottled body, kept.

Nothing redeems me. Today, I played a part in the city clearing
an overgrowth of trees near the library. The trees often hid a man sleeping

or doing something else you or I might have done at home.
What's left: a volunteer oak with volunteer birds. Thin wrists hold the nest.

Fear of wisteria. Fear of towns without interstates. Desire, not curiosity,
charts my migration. I acquired a passport for the lover

because how long can I love anyone my mother has not met?
Ten years. I listen to my heart at work and decide on anticipation not anxiety.

This is a fortune-teller heart. Mayoral candidates and their children lean over
my fence as I harvest melons. The lover shakes spiderweb from his face.

I observe everything animal. I don't tell you
anything animal. Even now, you might think less of me.

2

I want to go home, which is a concession—home isn't here. The opposite of possibility, to give up possession. I often think I am losing ground.

When the passport office closes, I cut my hair.

The passport office opens. I grow it out again.

It is possible what belongs to me doesn't dictate where I belong.

Once, at the beginning of an important friendship, we pointed at our flag and joked, *Can either of us write anything sincere about that?*[1]

---

1 *(Attempt)*

A flag can be colorized as a second flag to represent the smallest
faction of people or to celebrate a holiday or to make a statement
—and the flag is still recognizable but now means the United States
during Breast Cancer Awareness Month or the United States
of Police Officers or the United Colonized State as Mark Twain
once described, proposing a flag for my mother's country,
We can have just our usual flag, with the white stripes painted
black and the stars replaced by the skull and cross-bones.
Of course, my country is my mother's country. She insists, love both!

TONIGHT, A WOMAN

Asked not to put language in the garden

I could not.

Tonight, a CNN reporter was arrested when an officer refused to hear her credentials. He repeatedly asked, *Do you speak*

English. Now I fear I may be told I

speak nothing.

Ignore everything I have said about care.

I say it twice to negate.

I have heard someone I love speak around someone I love, like English is a sieve for catching one another's cruelty.

Catch and hold.

If people keep saying they love me

maybe they love me

and don't know what else to say.

The earth is an emotional wreck.

The earth is Eden + sin.

We are alive in an era of firsts we don't recognize. A coworker takes an ugly photo of me in my favorite dress, and I have no redemption arc.

Only a lovely speech pattern.

I had tried to say something about the garden. I had tried to say something about myself.

Plants that grow like weeds are popular cultivars.

We know the aftermath.

IN THE TRADITION OF WOMEN WHO'VE BLESSED ME TO TRANSFER THEIR VIRTUES

I give you what I don't have.
Strawberries in the mouths of birds.

Unopened pomegranate blossoms
devoured by ants. Fruit dropped

from unpollinated vines. Tell me
the last time a flower wasn't the shortcut

to desire. One year in the middle
of my life I asked, *How full do I want to be?*

Like hunger in the years before,
I asked fullness to be endless.

Every noise, I gave cause to.
An excuse to find comfort

in the sound of eating,
the small soul cutting a summer lawn.

I hear the thrum and wait
in my hothouse for dinner

to line up petal to petal,
plant fruit I've germinated

in my own mouth. Let the animal in.
I mean to say I'm in love

with that small mouth.
But I can't call love out

without telling the difference
between one mouth in the grass

and another. Permission is a fruit
I've cut from the tree, meaning

I've taken human sacrifice.
When I say, *be careful,*

I use your hands
in place of my hands.

When I feed the animals
the rabbit stands up

so straight she falls over.
That is the part I want

you to know. We are
that kind of animal.

TO SOMEONE WHO'S SAID *I LOVE YOU* TOO MANY TIMES

I understood the risk of it. The sound that alters
my heart. The sound I could not make
for myself. My mother didn't want me to repeat
her life. She wanted me to recognize
the possibility of repetition.
This year, she takes no photographs. Then
a friend photographs us in the woods. My mother
loves the possibility of the image.
At mall reflexology, she confesses
to a specialist the exact way work worries
her body. Mom says reflexology makes one thirsty
and overly confident. On the drive back,
she calls her husband to convey how she has chosen
a week with me over a week alone.
When my partner leaves for work, she asks,
Is it unusual for him to say, I love you*?*

THE WORLD BEGS FOR TRANSCRIPTION

My mother leaves a voicemail asking I work back-of-house when I can.

I haven't had a parent call afraid for my safety since 9/11.

Close to where I live, a couple books a hotel, purchases paramilitary gear, pays off a credit card, in order to hinder my life. The news refrains from describing the white couple's terrorist act at the Capitol. I wonder if it's not a question of the act but who feels it. Who has a good way to respond?

I'm going to distract you.

Nanay calls on Monday night to try out her new tablet. She alternates between *I'm beautiful* and *you're beautiful*. Beauty, meaning a pair.

We admit to gaining weight, and Ate Bernnie congratulates my well-attended Zoom meeting.

(Lots of repetition.)

Nanay wants to show that her hair is all white.

I've yet to find a term of self-reference that does not equate to ornament.

Someone I don't know mispronounces my name—worse—someone who would like to know me.

Be good and kind, they say, *or else*. But I am not good or kind or else I would not look for retribution.

Cardinals and squirrels before summer when I don't want to be responsible for their nests.

On a podcast, a poet I love names the many accountability groups she's joined this year. I am jealous of her self-discipline and the word *accountability*, used as a term of self-discipline, but that is not what I want.

I insist on protection. Pick up an omen the last night of the year. Foremost sin in my mind, the one not worth confessing.

Beloved, if it is the year of the comet, do not look for the comet.

I stay so long in one place my hair lines the nests. I don't know how to hold down what I love, but I've eaten so much fruit trying to lure the animal to me.

I go to the grocery store. Two men open the door for me.

I cannot stop them.

YONDER

Light breaks the window. You don't recognize light
as a hard hitter. Moonlight moonlighting as meteorite,
curtain rod come loose, cabinet collapsed at dawn, a sign
you must go out into the world, received by the reproduction
of gardenias and orange blossoms hungry for visitors.
Love bends the balcony in water weight. Once,
a neighbor cried out for help, collapsed under the collapsed
trellis of passionflowers. Maybe the best omen
for moderation is the thing we love pinning us down.
I check the value of my house on Zillow. My house moonlights
as a more expensive house online. Even the comfort of numbers
scares me. Then there is the comfort that the end of us isn't the end.

I HEAR THE MOON RATTLE, TOOTH LOOSE FROM THE GUN

On your side of the dreamscape we spend the night in a waiting room reading subtitles.

On my side, you cut my bangs perfectly with garden secateurs.

I deadhead roses to my own height in the new p.m. of daylight savings. Easy-care varieties of difficult flowers, like a crossbreed of two roses, which is still a hybrid, though both parents are roses.

(I believe there is some shameful memory here.)

Overnight, a man travels through multiple counties professing desire.

Being public-facing, I can't help but think of how often I offer assistance and am asked to gratify.

(Yesterday, a man who voted against integration told me I remind him of his wife, *a real lady*. Still, I helped him. I feigned interest for his advice regarding whom I could marry.)

The news hesitates to mention hate after the gunman's confession. They recount a man *lashing out* as police insist on his insistence, *he had not targeted victims, six of whom were of Asian descent, because of their race.*

I spend an hour getting dressed in clothing appropriate for a grief no one will recognize.

All my gestures reduce to desire.

And still, I have time

to say that the dreamscapes we recount are connected. When the moon isn't anything but two leaves unfolding for a fortnight. What have you got on you in that moment of exaltation?

Substitute desire now in each previous recitation.

MORE THAN HALF OF AMERICANS CAN'T NAME AN ASIAN AMERICAN

Which means I can do whatever I want without consequence?

I tell Nanay, I don't want a shirt that says "walang problema." Maybe because I'm walang hiya. Shame is a human emotion I have a lot of questions about.

In my twenties, I learned that shrimp in jambalaya is very Filipino. Making ppl mad about whom you date is very Filipino. At the Fil Am social, white wives are historically more accurate than white husbands. Morro Rock is infinitely larger than Plymouth Rock. The way a volcanic plug is less prone to erosion. The way some settlements aren't enshrined in reenactment. Because I couldn't name any inventions by Asian Americans, Nanay pointed out every Filipino. She claimed for me without patent: the durable manila folder, hemp rope, karaoke, butterfly knives, butterfly sleeves, three Disney princesses, smocking and pleating, lost continents, moon and stars,

and then there are those inventions made because we exist: the Santo Niño de Cebú (otherwise marketed as POC Jesus), American colonial expansion, the automatic pistol, American subjects without American passports, babies born on American bases who don't become American citizens, American soldiers who aren't American citizens. You can work so long for a country and never get SSI benefits.

Making

is very Filipino. historically more

infinite than

settlement re

invention in every

Filipino. She claimed me

pleating continents, moon and stars

because we exist

otherwise marketed as the

automatic subjects babies

born American who become American

o r n Ame n t You can work

In every pin-pleated aesthetic,
I become an ornament of you.

3

I request Tagalog Whitman via the State Library and Archives of Florida to be forwarded from the Los Angeles Public Library. I express how N. Gajudo's translations might help me reach outside this century where my nanay goes viral, and I'm last to find out, unable to vote in the election where Nanay waves two flags.[2]

---

2 *(Attempt)*

I've raised a flag only once at a small public library where I tried
to bring the flag in before rain & to take it down at night
because we had no exterior light. I sang a little song, not an anthem.

TO SOMEONE WHO'S HEARD *I LOVE YOU* TOO MANY TIMES

She asks, *Is it unusual for him to say,* I love you? At work
she analyzes the millennial affection for the multiverse,
sleep routines, and parental approval. She does not like
Everything Everywhere All at Once. Clients escape
the present for the imperceivable present, and she insists,
Live in this world. Even now, I do not know
what my mother loves or whom. (Repeat this thought
as little as possible.) I think dogs made her happy
once, then progressively less happy. Now she dismisses
my obsessions: mending with a long needle,
the provenance of jewelry she lends me,
the happiness of short-lived animals. She asks our nanay
to pray the rosary for the impossible things I still want.

LISTENING TO THE STORM, STILL DISTANT VS. SPECIFIC RAIN ON THE BANANA LEAVES

I bring jam to share at work after an exit interview in which a colleague calls me *robotic, unbelievably kind.* I imagine that at an impressionable age she watched *Blade Runner* or *Cloud Atlas* or *Ghost in the Shell* or *Madame Butterfly.*

I watched *Soylent Green* at an impressionable age.

I try to be beautiful by eating jam straight from the jar. I make the jam to avoid the effects of apocalypse: plastic particulates in the salt, a short growing season, supply chain shortages.

I do this during two of the forty-eight consecutive hours I have to myself.

I must account for each of them.

//

A coworker tells me it's hard to stay in a good mood when she has four hundred hours of sick leave. She is dying, *even after twelve weeks.*

Twelve weeks being the bright line at which she must return to work or lose her insurance.

//

I want to avoid self-sacrifice.

//

Last week, I told my mom that I couldn't meet up in New Orleans. The only thing I can save is the date.

Instead of saying I still need her, I send tea and garden photos.

She sends café selfies with beignets.

Two weeks later, she texts from urgent care. They have no prescription for her, and she has so much to do.

//

I ask whether she would like me to be there with her. After all, I have four hundred hours of sick leave and isn't that the point of FMLA?

Then I find out that is not the point of FMLA.

//

At work, the security guard insists I use the honorific, *Officer*, in written reports.

//

It isn't like the movies, this world. Someone can run for safety and show love.

I delay telling my boss, I can live or work, but I don't want to do both.

I write down twelve projects I might complete this year for additional income.

I decide to pay off my credit card.

When two coworkers die suddenly, nothing stops.

DURING THE STORM, THE CITY REASSURES ME

By reporting the number
of staff on standby
I am also on standby, ready
to reopen the office.
Which means I have time
to list the conditions
that would make me happy.
Overnight, the landscape shifts
under a new slip
as gossamer
as the words *I'm lucky.*
I dislike how a phone tree
has no roots and starts
from a radial center.
This is obvious,
but there's no way to talk back
to the heart of it. The heart
is a list of demands
I answer one by one.

ABUNDANCE

A downpour.

Which insists   Thursday   will not be consumed by the thousand

        accumulated tasks.   *Task today:*

            Planned Parenthood advises stocking up responsibly on Plan B.

Which means   leaving   something for others.

After a meeting,   someone leaves the office without

        saying goodbye.

A coworker sinks her teeth   into something she can't finish, and

I'm unwilling to eat after her   or throw out   what we both want.

Is it petty to cry over such things?

                The soft powder on plums
                and blueberries and grapes.

Which is wild yeast   identifying fresh

                unbothered fruit.

I want to name the part of me
                which denotes how long it has been

since I left home.

Or the part that reestablishes domicile.

For every poem

in an office in a garden

I want to know about property.

Who owns it?

Who tends it. Is this fruit stolen. Now

or in the next stanza?

I shake ants from me

but not as gently as I can.

I have lost patience, even

for this.

I'M NOT HERE TO SPEAK UNTIL YOU FEEL CLARITY

Questions I muted when I lost power:
How long does a hurricane last? Why haven't you evacuated?
Why is it called a rainband; is rain going on tour?

Frequently, I wanted to accuse those who asked the wrong questions.

//

After the second hurricane in as many weeks,
my insurer sent me an email inscribed, *This can be easy.*

The Washington Post informed me, I needed foreign-born workers
to rebuild the American Southeast at a good price.

//

I learned this from the radio years ago:
If you rest your hand above your heart it's harder to hate your body.

//

Ways I processed questions in a crisis—

//

I wedged my nail
under the calyx: ants, earwigs, jumping spiders,
bright beetle shells that reflected stove light.

//

I drank warm S. Pellegrino and failed to photograph the fluorescent blue

flashes illuminating the kitchen.
I was obsessed over language
of loss: The houses were not *gone* but *flooded.*

IF I ALLOW YOU TO LOOK INTO MY BLAMELESS DISASTER, WHOM DO YOU LOOK AWAY FROM?

Distinguish ordinary uncertainty from concerning uncertainty.
These feelings are interchangeable,
but what about meaningful uncertainty? Passive: My skin breaks
out at the beginning of every season.
Passive: I read my insurance policy and feel some sense of safety is possible.
Between storm surge videos, my father-in-law
sleeps with fluorescent life vests, which like persimmons are in season.
Unlike persimmons, their bright vermilion floats.
I test this. A persimmon sinks in my water glass. I talk to a friend
late into the night, before the internet cuts off.
No one can tell me why my father-in-law stayed until the bridges closed
and his couch floated out to sea.
The past tense would make us look foolish. Faith attenuated like silk.
Do I need to tell you how strong this fabric is, or
how it was rendered from sleeping bodies? It's difficult to name anyone
in this kind of production scheme,
but rendering generally refers to sustained heat and the extraction
of organic elements. So much change happens
while I'm asleep. *I'm almost forty*, I tell friends who are forty
so that they can open for me a five-year window
of productivity. Under the calyx of a persimmon I find unwanted surprises.

4

Nanay tells me about her new party's hashtag (#Kakampink). When the photographer came, she was crossing the street with my older cousin, handing out pink flyers and fans for the 2022 presidential campaign of Leni Robredo. I am in her sight lines. If I hold her gaze, we can pretend no decision will make us lonely.[3]

---

3 *(Attempt)*

We watch Uncle Egai paint a pink dove on the roof
so everyone in the barangay knows we are still People Power;
how Uncle Egai has always painted doves
as a symbol of revolution and god
and rebirth; how once he painted my face
to look like all the women who love me.

MAYBE THE BODY IS A LOVED ONE

Even the Chimera has siblings and children
she resembles. Her lover has a hundred
minds, all of them snakes that emit
fire and every kind of noise. Her children
come out almost all lion, barely any snake,
no remaining goat. Her daughter
speaks and has human breasts. But sits
like a four-legged creature. She conceives
questions instead of children, so want is some
undeveloped skill that mirrors the skills she has.
If asked to describe the Sphinx, we're given
the limbs. From animals, she sits at the dining table
with one leg up on the chair, knee to chest.

PANTOUM FOR LOLO AHAS

Thinking about proximity and trajectory.
Lolo takes a jeepney to the hospital for antivenom then
comes home with the imprint of a lizard's mouth.
The rest of his life, Lolo's called the thing he feared most.

Lolo takes a jeepney to the hospital and hears there's no poison
each time my uncle mentions a snake. My mother translates,
the thing he feared most. The rest of his life,
even when he avoids them, he sees curses.

Each time my uncle mentions Lolo Ahas, my mother translates,
who walked though the field with bare ankles.
I see curses everywhere. Even when I avoid them,
another springs up, familiar and willing to give me advice.

Through the field with bare ankles, I've walked
home to the imprint of a lizard's mouth
familiar and willing to give me another spring. I'd be kinder
if I felt more confident in my own ability to move quickly.

MY UNCLE'S ENGLISH IS DIRECT AND TO THE POINT

Specific about reservations and chanterelle mushrooms.
When I want dalagang bukid, he knows her name
in all the relevant languages and the name of a man
in Seattle who sells goldband fusilier. When he wants
to sound kind, my uncle calls me to explain whom he must
let down easy, and the service he will or will not provide,
so I can comb through the many rejections of my life
for the best and most comforting language
because we are so, so grateful for the opportunity
you have brought to us and though we will not
be offering you our services this year, like every good
family in America we are currently taking steps
to expand our capacity in the upcoming term.

MY MOTHER SAYS I NEVER LEARNED LANGUAGE

Because she didn't want to speak to herself.
Which makes it sound like I have no language.
I know about noise, endlessly
human. The first thing I said today
was *welcome*. I woke up before anyone
else in my house and in one version
I say *welcome* to my own little animal
scampering to its breakfast
and in another I speak to open
the doors of the office. Both have happened.
Some days, the first thing I say is a decree:
French toast or *tea* or *I think we should go*
to Tas-T-Os, even if the donuts are fried at midnight
and wait in the window until dawn. I know for sure
I would have lost whatever my mother might have said
over her infant. I am also quiet and distrustful.
I have not learned to convey
anything more than meaning, and I think
when she says I never learned language
she worries I will be lonely. On the way back
from work I call Mom
to describe a new bag of rocks by the railroad
crossing. Someone else's
mysterious labor. I am envious of it,
a new bag every week. Cumulative. I want
that certainty and, perhaps, to know what's coming.

I WORRY MY MOTHER WILL DIE AND I WILL KNOW NOTHING

Sometimes, history is too beautiful to be believed.
Nanay sold gardenias wrapped in banana leaves

until dinnertime. Then she found
better ways to earn a living. Years later, at an

American restaurant, I'm mistaken for a waitress
wearing all my silk. An accident I knew in my body

like the pride I felt when my adult mother said
I have narrow feet. Mother warns me, *Nothing will*

change. I'm alive and you don't know anything.
It was winter when my mother spoke, apples

rolling in the back seat, the fragrance shifting off-
site under the great deterrent of rain. It's still winter,

with a brown leaf staining my work
slacks. I smell the tea olives working up

spring (or the luxury of that kind of thinking
in January) when I explain to another

that my lunch wasn't useful. All my life,
I've wanted to lie with my stomach to the grass.

I've wanted to eat from community gardens.
I wrote a lie I'll admit now. I didn't eat

the municipal fruit. I bought the Cosmic Crisp
over the Honeycrisp for a dollar surcharge because

I wanted extra shelf life. The last day of the week, I split
the apple to decide if it's for sharing or eating whole.

It's a luxury to have your hunger. I'm sure I don't need to
go back, but can we go back to the restaurant? I am laughing

with the woman at the table next to mine about the woman
who would have me serve while I celebrate. She was going

to eat one dish, and I've ordered five. You know
I'll still leave hungry because I don't tell you

what I eat. See the phoenix with its mouth and feet grasping
for two servings? I am where I come from.

TO SOMEONE WHO'S HEARD *I LOVE YOU* TOO MANY TIMES

I ask friends about the things that scare me
like, *Have I always been allergic to muscadines*
or is it normal to feel this itchy from the juice?
Do I need to include a warning: Dear reader,
please don't eat your allergens. Picture what
I'd lose if I stopped eating. Literally, the road
was called Empire. It was made of dirt and one spoke
led to the old Mouzon house with the cat perpetually
giving birth and eating its own young. The
other led to me. From the trail that led to the tree
that stood in front of the rotten two-story colonial,
I would recite, sticky with muscadines, what
Drew Barrymore said to Anjelica Huston, in *Ever After*:
You are the only mother I have ever known. Was there a time,
even in its smallest measurement, that you loved me at all?

IN FAIRY TALES DISOBEDIENCE HELPS YOU TRAVEL

Gives you legs, a winter coat,
a husband you cannot see until
you see him by candlelight
you made yourself
out of earthly ingredients:
rat fat and disbelief.
He thinks being known
is devastating. You can
chase him as a lion
or a bird—or whatever
Psyche did. You can kiss
a man to teach him
a lesson—or whatever Christine
did. You can choose
to obey one parent and not
another; Cinderella
being a pillar of obedience
obeys a god-king and goes
to the ball
on the backs of mice.
But her mixed obedience
makes her difficult to recognize.

APPARENTLY, MONARCHS WHO EMERGE FROM MY YARD EACH WINTER

forgo migration.

Like homeland is wherever has kept you.

A coworker asks if I am happy here

and I say it's different for me.

Belonging demands being caught in one another's borders.

T. calls my identity overpronounced, a reproduction of women he does not know.

I watch a YouTube video about bouillon cubes, and he wants to know who I am.

I don't fail to notice history.

I want to live where most people love me.

I cook meals I imagine loved ones eating.

At the airport

a message from T.'s mother says she's caught on,

You don't seem interested in learning anything from us.

A colleague walks a little faster

in the parking lot.

At the table

someone asks if I've lost my tongue.

5

Nanay explained once how property works.

Nena owned the house and Nanay owned the land. But when Nena lived in Paris, Nanay lived in the house, and when I visited, I thought Nanay painted every flower.[4]

4 *(Attempt)*

As a child, I would ask Nanay to sing the American Thomasite rhyme, *Red White and Blue, Stars Over You*. Which is a song demonstrating patriotism toward an occupying party (*Mama said, Papa said*) that eventually becomes a song celebrating new nationalism (*I love you!*). That was the house wisteria pulled inward. Nothing would eat it. No one could sell it.
It's too soon to mention this kind of distance and how it shapes us.

TO SOMEONE WHO'S HEARD *I LOVE YOU* TOO MANY TIMES

Who among us has not followed a pattern
devised by someone else? I ask Tita Nena how
she wrote during martial law. She tells me,
                                        Be brave. Stay safe. As for me,
I went underground. There is no comparison
except the comparison. *During those years*
the women's liberation movement gained ground in Asia, though
whether entering the labour market under such
circumstances may be construed as emancipation
is another question. When Tita Nena wrote this sentence,
half her sisters worked overseas. Those years,
she wrote underground, collected no SSI, left my nanay
with responsibilities. A friend says, *Tell me more,*
and I wonder if I'm particularly sensitive to this demand.
During those years, Nena's lover created effigies
for those who'd disappeared but without hands
or a head (almost like a costume). He'd create a white
space for the audience to insert themselves
                                        into a history they'd rather avoid.

WADING INTO THE RIVER BENEATH THE INTERSTATE

A germination space. Then, the glass
between what you love today and what you loved
yesterday. Vibrant, rich actions. Vibrant, rich

growth. After Eden, everyone goes home.
To plant seeds. To say we love the unrelenting
aspects of the world and carry them with us

into its aftermath, which is full of potential.
You are rebuilding the garden someone taught you
to love. Tucked into the erosion (The river at work.

At work, semitrucks above us. How do you decide
which of your parts you won't submerge in fresh water?)
on the bank, a bird rebuilds her nest above

the tideline. Mothers say happiness is inherited.
Sometimes the garden is made of stones.
Care first. Decide about love later.

AT THE ECOLOGICALLY ENGINEERED STORMWATER RETENTION BASIN

Cottonmouth sunning on a pine berm
after a loud shake in the leaves,
by shake I mean earth-shaking. Green
lizard after green lizard emptying
out of the forebay. I send a snapshot
to a friend who says, *Yes, that's a thick*
snake. I want to see more. The world
isn't miserably sad here. I expand
and live in the warm days. All April,
little sucking marks on blackberries,
popped seeds and filament in the shape
of a tiny mouth. Osmanthus flowers
kneeled into the oak hammock patrolled
by one worried cardinal. There is only
one egg in the bush. I think this is my fault.
I set an appointment for the first of May,
which is the earliest I can schedule
a subdermal birth control implant,
then ask everyone to visit me in June,
before Florida's most recent
legislative agenda takes effect.

AFTERNOON IN THE CEMETERY

under loblolly pines

I don't believe in hallowed ground, but I like that border control
doesn't come here. It's smelling season. I'm staring
at the wide eagles' nest because I would like an illegal feather,
when a woman's dog growls at my arrangement
low in the grasses. She says her dog never barks, so I avert my eyes
from the fledglings above. Like a secret
just past the blackberries' five-pointed stars. I could love this place
if I didn't know the reason for it.

under cherry blossoms

I'm a tourist. I debate whether the citizen star
on my ID is sufficient so close to the border.
In the end, I don't board a ferry to cross. I touch the end
of my hairpin to feel secured by what's expensive. I text a loved one
on the other end of the sound. Maybe I write an apology,
though to whom, it's too early to tell. To a friend, I admit,
given a second opportunity I'd record all my English
in italics. A formal decentering to ensure my mother's speech
is roman. The alternative document would offer
a shared experience, a poem that's *of the world*
but a world that's better for me. *Of course you don't love it.*

under coastal redwoods

Perhaps a poem can be better than the world
because of my obsessions. On weekends, after Mom bought
her first house, we'd watch *The Crow*, a movie in which the star
is Asian and white. My mother liked to point out which characters
I could grow into. "Not the Crow," she'd tell me
after Brandon Lee's last scene. I wonder how it is for others.
Mothers say, come visit, lovers say
come home, enemies say, go home. The line I remember
from the movie is not central to the story.

AFTER FLORIDA'S SIX-WEEK ABORTION BAN TAKES EFFECT

The mail courier comes to the door to say she's been watching
the peach tree for weeks, so I give her the fruit I'm most jealous of.
A friend's analysis: *You gave up a responsibility*
I think? Or you gave away your vice. Now it's delivered.
It's early May. I pick peaches in the dark by smelling the red cheek.
I think I could have kids like this. Probably the most mundane
thing to do in early summer. Everything right now feels heavier than it looks
and that's how I know it's time to eat. I take fruit to the airport
to sweeten my appeal, but really, I distribute the raw fruit
so I don't have to plan for the future. The airport
is on the other side of the forest. When I drive through at 4 a.m.
I can't distinguish the treetops from the night sky so the trees
take on an impossible height. I count 15 deer before I stop
counting. The most terrifying deer are the ones in motion—
doesn't matter if they're moving away from the road or toward it.

WARHEADS

She asks, *Are 200 peach pits not enough?* I say, *I could eat,*
though I've reached the point where any unripeness erodes my tongue.
Like the brand of candy we ate in the early 2000s and celebrated
for its total destruction, as we ourselves engaged in new warfare.
Then, I thought peach was not a possible Warheads flavor because
lemons and watermelon and apples are more transportable, more—
This week, the US Navy is engaged in live and inert bombing
in the Ocala National Forest, movements not far from where I live.
On Facebook, a man calls them "freedom seeds." Mine, too, is a comparison
that undercuts the exercise being prepared. Which is more violent?
The answer should be obvious, but I'm concerned lately
by how I grew up eating candy with a white head exploding
into a small mushroom cloud and how this is typical
of settler-colonial order—so much so that I don't recognize the bombs
as bombs but as something innocuous and natural, with a future.

ASSEMBLE THE MOCKINGBIRD

Almost certain
there is no living bird

minus nine feathers.
Every found object is evidence

of disenchantment.
The opposite is also true.

Say we walk in circles
like the night. The mockingbird

started with these
perfect feathers

lifted like any part of the body
should be unwilling to suffer.

LESSONS FROM THE REPLICANT

Yesterday a man shouted after me and input the syllabics of an animal command

to run: giddya— and hiyah—

I ran the longer route to the cemetery in response to his truck backing up. I don't think the single
incident is interesting. Everybody asks me to finish the thought

they won't [ ].

Egrets in the cemetery sway like the wind catches them

but muscles stabilize their eyes
to the branches they stalk.

I fantasize about interviewing the driver to determine if I'm white-passing.

(Should I account for his actions the other way? In combination?)

Reacting

and not reacting are both stereotypes. A momentary lapse in judgment. A flushed face

signifies [ ] about cause

but as a child I heard that my bloodlessness
meant I photographed best in winter.

For a short time in my twenties, I tried to like violent men.

They had a phrase, hurt

but no harm, which meant they committed
what everyone doled out for free.

All the bodily acts that suggest pleasure,

they're the tasks I'd most like to hand over to the machine.

In workshop [ ] inserts
[ ] as a spirit guide for [ ].

I consider volunteering
for the role and wonder if I would emphasize or dilute
authenticity.

[ ] boasts familiarity

with both kinds of [ ]

I might be. The first time I saw my likeness

on television, the actress pretended
to be all-white. The second time, she wasn't human at all.

LETTER TO MY YOUNGER SELF

When I see men digging clay beside the confederate
monument, I want to know if this is where we bury
unspecific history.

Lately, I worry. Today, I was told
most mixed-race women die in fiction, which implies
that the living version of myself is difficult

for others to imagine. Today a crossing light
swallowed by the rainy season joined the number
of things I've touched that fall into sinkholes. All space

I didn't know I was risking. I worry
about the unimportant ways you busy your hands.
Get thee to a dry cleaner, my love.

Let someone else play human. The woman behind me
can't stand to look. *Who could do that every day*, she says,
like each night I boil moths myself and spin silk.

DREAMSCAPE DRESSED IN MY YOUNGER SELF

First, you have a dress of gold, but
you can't wear it. The gold dress cannot
be washed or dry-cleaned. Hell, the tag
says no spot-cleaning. So you have a dress
of gold, just in case. Then a field of red sorrel
in rows like someone loves it. Then a pine
forest with a dogwood floor. Next the Perseids
behind sheet lightning. Next-year fruit
from your own cuttings. Slice me fruit
from the year I have yet to grow. I couldn't slice
a pomegranate with less than six cuts.
Once you learn, there's only one way to prepare
the pip-star in each soft pear. I have seen illustrations,
and I have been scolded by so many women
for making indefensible halves at their pie table. Now,
remember that dress we're saving. You try it on.

SUBDUCTION

I often think about what the South has to say adjacent to me.

The last time I was honest with my employer I explained
I was experiencing vertigo before coming to work.

When I left, a colleague inserted
an "i" into my name. The greeting card said she'd miss Asia.

When two continents rub together, usually,
one converging plate will move beneath the other. Yes, I

feel shame but not regret.

Dealing with other people, my father told me,
convince them there is a version of the world in which they give you what you want

for nothing. There is another version
in exchange where you labor twice as much. Double or nothing. Yes.

There is something I want.
The moon rises 50 ft. over the tallest thing I've planted.

6

Three weeks after my interlibrary loan request, I'm notified Tagalog Whitman can't leave LA.

May the lulls between revolutions be filled with progress like a daughter who writes poems. May she report the more mutable nature of her friends and employers. In the National Gallery, I am selfish about the art I want to see. I cannot remember if Nena is known to Egai in 1974. Will the artist abandon abstraction before or after meeting Nena? This is my favorite moment in art. My aunt enters the painting. The artist moves toward realism to render her face. How close are these intimacies?

It's so hard to write about love without writing about the country we live in.

TO SOMEONE WHO'S HEARD *I LOVE YOU* TOO MANY TIMES

Your friend explains having been in a room
filled with other people who, like you and your friend,
collect words from parents. The words
[   ]
don't come together into a language.
And the person on the stage expressed deep shame
for a project where she had tried to speak
but misspoke in a language
for which she had no teacher.
This is what you most fear. In one language,
you are the perpetual infant. You point to the moon
and call it payneta moon, once every 28 days.
Nanay gave you what is specific. Not the general
name for the moon [   ].
                                  Everything you say
timing and intimacy have shaped.

AFTERIMAGE

My ex is an institution who wants me back.

The institution is a safe space

encompassed by a larger, heterogeneous space.

Implied: that the mix is safe

and unsafe. Safe and undefined. Undefined and clear-

and-present-danger. It's important to say I fear for my life

if I'm to lend my complaints credibility

later. *Who's left? Who misses me at the office?*

Credibility demands I stay in love.

Thinking of ordering a new dress. Something

country club to wear in the code-red air.

I don't want to impress people.

I want to survive them. I show pictures of my parents

to shock and deflect. Today I sewed the unhewn cuff

of my lover's shirt with an imperfect

seam. After a Zoom meeting, he folds the shirt

to interpret my work as finished. This is what the mirror

self thought I would not do or, if I did,

I would not do imperfectly.

My own relationships don't shock me. The dream that stays

with me is someone else's but about me. In his dream,

the black half of my rabbit's coat has turned

white from cold. The rabbit is all white,

and in the dream logic whiteness precedes death.

IF YOU AREN'T EXPLICIT, THEY'LL SAY YOU NEVER MENTIONED THE WAR

My newsfeed is all about babies.
Helen is so tired and so relieved;
her baby born a few weeks early.
The Blue Ridge Mountains are full
of weaned opossum. The wildlife
rescue continues to tell me who
survives, who passes. Even
the dead have news. *This little*
whydah passed the next day.
He was warm and comfortable.
In all the photos are living animals.
It's early fall. In the video
of a hospital press conference, a man
on the ground by the podium holds
a baby. I look closely and ask Instagram
to suggest fewer posts about god
and motherhood. I'm most
likely to like a photo of a wild animal
because I fear what the algorithm
will bring. God, the babies.

ALL CONVERSATIONS THAT MAKE THEIR WAY INTO DISASTER FAIL TO HOLD UP THE STAKES OF LIVING

Even conversations about disaster.

I order stationery when shipping throughout the Southeast is fucked. I resist making an offer of housing to unhoused in-laws. But I invite a friend off the internet to live with me. When the county announces a "no-flush zone," everyone has work through another state and a teammate who hasn't the bandwidth for another delay. Someone's toddler rejoices in her temporary reprieve from the toilet. She pees all week in the grass. I had not imagined a god-gaze separate from a eurocentric-gaze. Wine and cake are plentiful. At the party, everyone takes turns in the self-driving car, which attempts to overcome sand dunes and appliances along the assigned route. The beach is closer than ever and what we all love. Even now, someone admits. The world we don't safeguard, probably stays.

I ACCEPT ALL MEASURES OF INTIMACY IN THE DIGITAL AGE, ESPECIALLY TEXT

The way, sometimes, I find comfort looking
away from you, having leaned over your shoulder
to examine, this hour, oak canopies
or in the other direction, indigo milk caps,
tussock caterpillars, silk threads (not that kind
of silk and, yes, that kind). Empty cocoons
are lucky, and incomplete cycles are sad
but not a bad sign. There's nothing I must avoid
seeing. Once, I buried a dead squirrel alongside a live
flatworm. Once, I tried to convince vultures
to move a carcass off my roof. At the sheriff's office,
there's an isolated, signal-less room
that's directly linked to staff turnover at the public
defender's office. You tell me, not what you've seen
but what you've confirmed. Maybe it's a good sign
when videos entered into evidence are grainy
recordings from the '80s. I can believe in good intentions.
These woods were a field in the '80s. Now they're a study
on reforming forests. Returning from the
forty-year-field, you overtake my position so that
as the taller of us, you'll catch all the silk
and I'll emerge unbothered by skin irritants, spurge
and stinging nettle. That morning, when I complained
about the carcass on our roof, I texted that I was shocked
and sad but I hoped that the vultures would stay
focused on cleanup. You couldn't receive my messages.
So what you first read was my disbelief. *Bald eagle,*
bald eagle! At some point, this poem was about desire.
I think it still is.

THE LITTLE RED HEN

We straddle a fence enclosing //// ///////

/// / / /// /

/////////

a stranger's field until that crime of proximity.

I quit my job. HR sends a volunteer form.

I don't know how much

their recommendation hinges on my continued availability.

The field is full of wheat until /////
//
/ / /
/
/

At my last job the director couldn't stand the question,

Who will eat the bread?
To teach compassion

as a last resort. Weekends laminated croissants in my own kitchen

and rationed them like h/ours/

I consume my past self or feed her to others.

I love most what Little Red Hen says to the animals.

She's honest about what she wants.

This morning.

Which smells flat and sweet and lonely, not at all like bread?

I love it for someone else.

Who will eat this bread?

I am showing off an ability for recklessness.

No, you won't.

TOYO

Early in the supply shortages, I began to make my own miso. I grew soybeans (I could not buy them), then aged them with salt and koji I ordered online. After eleven months, the toyo, skimmed from the top, was a surprise byproduct. My loved ones point out that the sea is rising and old regimes have returned to power. It's not an excuse anymore, to say the apocalypse moves slowly. When I came home from Quezon City, I had lost ten pounds. I took steroids to heal my ears, damaged from consistent flight. I experienced stress-induced eczema. Skin blistered and peeled away from my hands and feet. My lover coddled me distinctly so nothing might press against the ears or brush my hands. At dinner, he separated tinik from meat to make a moderate offering by my rice. I was happy for a way to show that what I described as suffering, could be ocular suffering. In the mountains, at each curve in the road, there is someone with a flashlight. The work is self-appointed, to direct drivers away from the precipice. They save us from the cliff and they shine their lanterns into our eyes. It is so difficult to write a poem about the ways people might find me credible and also admit to *having toyo*. When Dickinson asserts *I measure every Grief I meet*, she is also 32 and definitely has toyo, but she acknowledges the suffering of others. Because I'm in the middle of a city, I can grow heirloom without much Monsanto, so the miso I age in Lolo's crock is whole and worth the eleven months he lived in this country believing I would eat well, fill up on vegetables and become president. Being salty makes my ears feel better. Today, I told a friend in my kitchen that I had added two spoonfuls into her dish and she heard teaspoons. She worried about measurement and I worried I could not enunciate. Which is no big deal except when it is. I wanted to warn her about tinik but I didn't want to say tinik and I didn't want to translate bone into smaller bone. I had already translated this dish into miso soup when it's really a variation of sinigang. Everything about me is an affect of failed language. The metaphor is a sign I'm lonely. So you can hear me better.

(FR)I(E)NDEX

Thank you all for our conversations. My favorite lines are always yours.

1. Rhoni Blankenhorn
6. Elise Deming, Namita Gupta
13. Sokunthary Svay
19. Rhoni Blankenhorn
38. Pamela K. Santos
40. Carolina Hotchandani, Amy Martinelli, Meredith Poisson, Jimin Seo
49. Annie Wenstrup
55. Rhoni Blankenhorn
56. Shelby Handler, Laura Cresté, Sara Mae, Ally Ang
57. C. E. Janecek
58. Jimin Seo, E. Hughes, Sarona Abuaker
60. Jimin Seo
69. Paula McCahon, Erin Arnold, Suzanne Brown, Sindy Sato, Cy Butler
71. Annie Wenstrup
74. Helen Hua
75. Erin L. McCoy
79. Ted Riquelme

NOTES

The first epigraph is from Gina Osterloh's 2022 presentation at the Yale School of Art, "Representation & Identity, Illusion & the Real," and references Roger Caillois's 1935 essay "Mimicry and Legendary Psychasthenia," translated into English in 1984 by John Shepley.

"In 1981, Tita Nena Translates Whitman" (in section 1) references Nena Gajudo Fernandez's *Sa Labi ng Iba— : Mga Tula sa Pagsasa* (1981), which includes a translation of Whitman's "For You O Democracy" from *Leaves of Grass*. In section 6, the painting is *Give and Let Live* (1974), an early work by Filipino social-realist painter Edgar Talusan Fernandez. The prompt italicized in section 2 is from Sokunthary Svay.

Thank you to Aimee Nezhukumatathil for helping shape "Certain Outlines Can Only Be Imagined."

In "I'm Interested in How Animals Teach Us Pleasure," the plums are from Penryn Orchard, the hair clips are from Chunks.

"Disagreeable Aspects of Hyphenation" ends with an altered quotation from *Star Trek*, season 1, episode 2 of the original series.

"Tonight, a Woman" refers to Minnesota State Patrol's violent and unlawful arrest of CNN producer Carolyn Sung in April 2021.

"The World Begs for Transcription" was originally published as "Now vs. When Lilacs Last in the Dooryard Bloom'd." Written in response to the attack on the United States Capitol on January 6, 2021, the poem reflects on Walt Whitman's "When Lilacs Last in the Dooryard Bloom'd," an elegy for a nation in mourning.

"Yonder" begins with a line adapted from William Shakespeare's *Romeo and Juliet,* act 2, scene 2.

"I Hear the Moon Rattle, Tooth Loose from the Gun" includes a quotation from a March 17, 2021, *New York Times* article, "At Least 8 People Killed in Atlanta-Area Massage Parlor Shootings."

"More Than Half of Americans Can't Name an Asian American" is a burning haibun, after torrin a. greathouse.

In "Listening to the Storm, Still Distant vs. Specific Rain on the Banana Leaves," FMLA stands for the Family and Medical Leave Act, which in the United States provides certain employees with up to 12 weeks of unpaid, job-protected leave per year.

In "To someone who's heard *I love you* too many times [Who among us has not followed a pattern]," the sentence in italics is from Nena Gajudo Fernandez's "The Philippines: Dissent of the Migrant Women," published in *Women, Violence and Nonviolent Change* (World Council of Churches, 1996), edited by Aruna Gnanadason, Musimbi Kanyoro, and Lucia Ann McSpadden.

In "Wading into the River Beneath the Interstate," "vibrant, rich actions" is a line borrowed from Samiya Bashir's September 26, 2023 *VS* podcast interview, "Samiya Bashir vs. Multiple Mediums." Thank you to Shelby Handler for introducing me to Poet's Beach, where this poem was written.

“At the Ecologically Engineered Stormwater Retention Basin” borrows “I expand and live in the warm day” from Emerson’s *Nature* and a text message from C. E. Janecek.

“After Florida’s Six-Week Abortion Ban Takes Effect” includes advice from Jimin Seo.

“Assemble the Mockingbird” includes a line altered from Lord Byron’s “She Walks in Beauty.”

“Letter to My Younger Self” references “Letter Four” in Paisley Rekdal’s *Appropriate: A Provocation*.

“Afterimage” is very loosely after Jericho Brown’s duplex form.

“If You Aren’t Explicit, They’ll Say You Never Mentioned the War” references Israel’s acts of genocide in Gaza. The italicized text is from the Ventura Hummingbird Rescue’s Instagram, dated October 21, 2023. The title is in response to a fact from Karen Dandurand’s research on Dickinson that I obsess over: three of the ten poems published during Emily Dickinson’s lifetime appeared in *The Drum Beat* to raise funds for the Union Army.

“Toyo” references Emily Dickinson’s “I measure every Grief I meet” (550) from *The Poems of Emily Dickinson: Reading Edition* (Belknap Press of Harvard University Press, 1999), edited by R. W. Franklin. The poem was likely written during the Civil War.

CREDITS

A few of the poems in this collection also appear in the chapbook *One Way to Listen* (Gold Line Press, 2023). The following journals have published individual poems, sometimes in earlier versions.

The Adroit Journal: "I Worry My Mother Will Die and I Will Know Nothing," "Tonight, a Woman," and "Toyo"

The American Poetry Review: "Pantoum for Lolo Ahas" and "Yonder"

Copper Nickel: "I'm Interested in How Animals Teach Us Pleasure," "To someone who's heard *I love you* too many times [She asks, *Is it unusual*]," and "To someone who's said *I love you* too many times"

Epiphany: "If You Aren't Explicit, They'll Say You Never Mentioned the War"

The Georgia Review: "Apparently, Monarchs Who Emerge from My Yard Each Winter" (as "*from* Tonight, a Woman"), "Disagreeable Aspects of Hyphenation," "During the Storm, the City Reassures Me," "I Hear the Moon Rattle, Tooth Loose from the Gun" (as "T. and I Compare the Dreamscape"), "I'm Not Here to Speak Until You Feel Clarity," and "The World Begs for Transcription" (as "Now vs. When Lilacs Last in the Dooryard Bloom'd")

Honey Literary: "In 1981, Tita Nena Translates Whitman"

Kundiman South Zine: "At the Ecologically Engineered Stormwater Retention Basin"

Michigan Quarterly Review: Mixtape: "Abundance" and "Listening to the Storm, Still Distant vs. Specific Rain on the Banana Leaves"

ONLY POEMS: "After Florida's Six-Week Abortion Ban Takes Effect," "Maybe the Body Is a Loved One," and "Wading into the River Beneath the Interstate"

Poet Lore: "Lessons from the Replicant" and "Subduction"

Poetry: "To someone who's heard, I love you, too many times [The couple who owns the restaurant that makes]" and "To someone who's heard, I love you, too many times [Who among us has not followed a pattern]"

Poetry Northwest: "Heirloom" and "Letter to My Younger Self"

Sierra: The Magazine of the Sierra Club: "Certain Outlines Can Only Be Imagined"

Southern Humanities Review: "Dreamscape Dressed in My Younger Self"

Tupelo Quarterly: "In the Tradition of Women Who've Blessed Me to Transfer Their Virtues"

VOLT: "Afterimage"

"I Worry My Mother Will Die and I Will Know Nothing" was selected by Ada Limón for episode 520 of *The Slowdown*

"In the Tradition of Women Who've Blessed Me to Transfer Their Virtues" was anthologized in *The Best of Tupelo Quarterly* (2023), edited by Kristina Marie Darling

"Toyo" was reprinted by *Poetry Daily*

ACKNOWLEDGMENTS

If a stanza is a room, we choose who enters. A poem is a gathering, and I'm so thankful to the friends and mentors who have entered these rooms with me.

Originally I had written a list of personal acknowledgments expressing gratitude to institutions, teachers, friends, loved ones, and those who raised me. And then I realized because of the current political climate of the United States, I did not feel comfortable listing with specificity the names of those who raised me. Who, in an act of gratitude, would risk the safety of a loved one? And in what kind of country might an explicit expression of love be a risk? Every book I write after this one will necessarily address a nation that imagines the body as a border crossing. (Today, I am writing this as a reaction to a memo that may tomorrow become a law.) Given that my acknowledgments cannot be complete, I offer instead a promise. Any home that makes me feel unsafe naming my loved ones, is a home I will reinvent. The United States is a home I write towards remaking.

I've said "I love you," so many times in this book, and yet I've never written "Mahal kita." Mahal ko kayo'ng lahat. Maraming salamat.

ASA DRAKE is a Filipina/white poet in Central Florida. A 2024 National Poetry Series finalist, she is the recipient of fellowships and awards from the 92Y Discovery Poetry Contest, the Florida Book Awards, the Rona Jaffe Foundation, Storyknife, Sundress Publications, Tin House, and Idyllwild Arts. Her poems have been published with *Poetry*, *The Slowdown* podcast, *The American Poetry Review*, and *The Georgia Review*. A former librarian, she currently works as a teaching artist.